SOUL_AR

Chioma Hasan

BookLeaf Publishing

Presentation by *BookLeaf Publishing*

Web: www.bookleafpub.com

E-mail: info@bookleafpub.com

ISBN: 9789357441384

First edition 2023

TO MY MOM AND DAD FOR CREATING ME.

TO THE PEOPLE I LOVE AND LOVED.

TO THE HIGHER BEAN NURTURING ME.

& TO ME FOR NEVER GIVING UP.

H.O.P.E (How On Planet Earth)

How On Planet Earth
Did I get this way
Time in the car
leave or stay?
Can't Blame Them
For Believing what Naive say

Naive was my friend
She taught me
That I
could believe the words of any
Plenty times i tried this gesture
Many time i cried for alone

Alone was my Mother
She taught me that the feeling of self
Was never madness
Just a dealing of knowledge
That being with self
Means it's okay to leave Alone

Self was my husband
We laughed cried and tried together
He taught me

That know matter what happens
Look for him in ever which way
And don't let lust fool me again

Lust was my lover
The feeling of him made me forget self
He taught me
That pain don't last forever
But the feeling still flows in my brain

Pain was my drug
Somehow I misuse it
when I wanted to feel numb
It taught me
That this feeling
Will come every time I wasn't with happiness

Happiness was my baby
I tried to hold on
But self saw me suffocated it
My baby taught me
To cherish time carefully

Time was my personality
It formed the ways of life
that taught me
Just because I keep choosing right and wrong
Life was never going to stop for me or these emotions

Life was my home
Comfortable. But tragic
Every time I lay in life
It makes me notice that
Self and happiness wants to stay
but my choices makes them go away

How On Planet Earth
Did it get this way
Take me back to life
So i can make this right.

PLANET HEARTBREAK.

I wish you could've warmed me with those hugs
And filled hot chocolate in my mug
Giving me a life that I had to take
Some much pain for a girl my age
My siblings were were tormented
But we had to stay
On this place called Planet Heartbreak

Mama Mama
You don't know how much
Your children cried for you
Daddy Daddy
Don't you know how much
Your children lied for you
If death did us apart its
Because I died for you
Jail Cell gave you pain
That left you awake
Drug sells kept less rain and more estates
I don't complain because
I was reborn on Planet Heartbreak

I manage to love and hate myself altogether
I gave myself so much mystery
That personality I sold myself was misery

And he never loved me thats how we became history
So don’t tell me to reach
Don’t tell me to wake
Don’t tell me to speak
Don’t tell me to pray
Don’t tell me to preach
Don’t you dare tell me about faith
Cause how I found GOD
Is way better then how I ended up on Planet Heartbreak

Yes, this journey took me a while
Once it was so bad
I started to walk for miles I stop and gathered trees
That’s numbered my loud
As I lied there
The wind smelt sour
I followed the scent and it lead me to a flower
It told me about a new phase
It called it Majichour
Trying to pull it out
It kept going downwards
I pulled it to the limit
That’s how I added power
Finally got it out
And it started a spring shower
I released a positive energy

That I never thought ill make
Knowing that this walk I’m going
Is for my own sake
In the end I learned to love the flaws and
rotation
On Planet Heartbreak.

when the sun goes down.

In the dark
I sit in dirt
It's starting to rub off
on my shirt
a Bullet went right through my hurt
I'm cursed
They said
It's gone get worse
They said
If I don't reach inside
My purpose bin
I tend to feel the seven chills
Of pain, love, lust, trust ,strength , wisdom and
trend

Cause in the dark
I do my dirt
Lobe to the devils whisper
"Come on it wouldn't hurt "
My reply
"I know it won't."

ACCEPT

I ACCEPT YOUR FLAWS
I ACCEPT YOUR SMILE
I ACCEPT THE HORRORS THAT CREATED HALF OF YOU
I ACCPET THOSE POW WOWS
WHEN WE TALK FOR HOURS THE DANCE AGAIN
THESE MEMORIES I SEE DONT FADE WITHIN
I ACCEPT YOUR TROUBLES
I ACCEPT THOSE LIES THE LITTLE WHITE ONES IN A DISGUISE
I ACCEPTS THE FUTURE THAT WE HAVE TIL THE END OF TIME
THANKS TO YOU I ACCEPT THE WORLD YOU THINK IS FINE
I WOULD STILL WANT YOU EVEN IF WE DIDN'T TIE
I ACCEPT THE LOVE I SEE IN YOUR EYES CAUSE YOUR SO KIND
MEALIN SKIN SO DEVINE
THE THOUGHT OF YOU TOUCHES MORE THEN MY HEART IT TOUCHES TIME
THE MORE IM WITH YOU THE MORE MY LOVE IS WISE

YOU KEEP ME SANE
CAN YOU BE MY LIFE LINE ?

fall.

I'm throwed off
But so are you
All we have to do is stay connected
Until the vines are loose
If we truly love like we say we do
Life is a jungle gym
That's Something we play through
I just want you to know
I can't stop
Wondering about you
If you were sick
How I will care for you
If you were lost
I will take your hand and guide you through
If you were in trouble
I will lie for you
If you couldn't do it
I will try for you
If you ever wanted to hide and cry
I will wipe your tears Nd lie on top of you
If you were hungry
I will share my last with you
If you had no funds to give
I will give you my all
if you fall

Remember You are not alone
Ill be there overall.

EVERYTHING+YOU.

I don't think y'all understand..
How a heart can be took
Stolen from its owner
And never to be seen again
Never to be touched again
Never to be held again

I don't think y'all understand
How the Vulnerable hurt
Tears stained like dirt
And never to be the sane again
Never to have a name again
Always walk ashamed within

I don't think y'all understand
When that tunnel gets dark
The deeper you go everything gets marked
And it never find its way again
Never see the worlds face again
Moving but passing the same place again

I really don't think y'all understand
That this isn't about love anymore
Or selling drugs at the store or being scared to leave the porch...

Its a mind thing
And it's better to stay a wise mane
Because while living in a time frame
Everything + You must go back to the Higher plane

say a little prayer.

DEAR GOD,

I'm writting to you to tell you how much pain
I'm in..
I'm praying to you, to confront my sins …
I met a men
Not a very popular one
The one that people toot there nose
at because he wasn't raised properly
Or his life isn't desirable

I love this man
This man I love
I know someday he'll love me back
But it's Ramadan and I have to keep my feelings
enact.
I'm asking you to give me a miracle
I mean something beautiful
And not love and sex
But another freedom chance
For both of us
This is dangerous

Cause I love this man
This man I love

Needs to know that your above
it was my father then now him
Now I'm extra strong for both of them
I need you to hear me
Please god hear me
The love that you carry for him is stronger then mines
God oh God
Listen to this prayer of mines

Cause I love this man
This man that I love
Has another family
His mother just want to hold him
If I could I would betrothed him
Just to keep him safe
I know I left but that's because He forgot my place
Didn't know if I was the enemy with a angel face
God oh God
Give him one more chance
Please I'll sacrifice whatever for romance

Cause I love this man
This Man I love
Keep him strong in that box
Tried my best to keep him from the cops
But your plan always come

In a strange way
Funny how I had to take a strange way
Funny how they caught him on a strange day
Baby let me know if your okay
God Oh God
What else can I say
We'll make a step
Just help us along the way.

for the love of sailing.

Im not a sell out
I just sailed out
Took a voyage through Atlantis
They say I'm small
Preying mantis
Watered myself
Learned to grow
Into a planet

I'm a hopeless romantic
It comes so frantic
I follow cause i'm enchanted
do I mind?
Sometimes..
Sometimes I ride on the thought of it
Sometimes I think..then marinate

I go so fast
Nd pass
the important places
It's not a race to me
They chase til the end
But I glide on the infinity

I met many people
Nd my only phrase is
You got a friend in me
Im on a journey with love
And it feel like 10 of me

Don't question My extortion
To this place
My heartbreak don't define me
When my goals change they surprise me
You might call it crazy
I call in perfect timing

I'm not a sell out
I just sailed out
Noticed the escape from pain
And got the hell out.

lucky planet # 7.

A month ago
You were in my arms
Sorrow dripping down
I'm calm
I don't think I ever felt a way so strong
Your soul is pulling from within my lungs
I wanna scream your name
An wither
these summer nights
Feel like winter
Where now in my blowup bed
I shiver
Grown a upper temper
In this sunny December
Memories of when we danced in the street
Finding a love
That won't proceed
I refuse to let this river
End this way
A consent struggle
Of missing you today
I don't wanna keep replaying
The happiness when I felt a way
Me without you don't feel like I'll make a place
God I don't need him more then I need you

But now I understand the meaning of two.
Arguments with you
Feel like wildfire
And making love feels like heaven
What am I supposed to do with you gone
In the wind
Please roll home
My lucky 7.

spring.

Spring is starting
And it's more rain then ever
Leaves and trees don't look the same anymore
Me and you won't change anymore
Well rather sit in a storm
Then realized where is coming from
I scream I hate you more than I forgive you
You hit me more than I bargain for
I want this to stop
So I won't go chasing waterfalls
But I'll still think about you
Cause that's Where the water calls
Your not my blood but I still treat you as such
Not Even wondering where it went wrong
Got me wondering what's our song
Before I even remember when we met
I still want you all along
I didn't know I broke your heart
Until I saw you
Dancing, laughing, and crying with her
You cheated repeatedly
And I cause a ruckus constantly
The day I left I sought out for help
You told me it wouldnt work
Instead of

it wouldn't hurt To take you with me
The time I spent alone
I written a song that would've made you and me happy..
something that would've saved you
When I felt the urge to try to find you
You was already happy
Made me notice who I was to you
I was never your savior
I was your nightmare
In realization..
Helding head down
Wishing I could be you
For a moment
You finally had that boy you wanted
A wife that greeted you at the door
Now tears are pouring
When you finally look at me
you see your Favorite thunderstorm
Not knowing how to speak
I left you with a smile that felt courageous for a new life
Rushing away from the door
I feel a new water wave
pulling me towards him
As I fell into oblivion
stumbled upon a grave
That read my name a then say
You are truly loved.

LIFE ON A ROCKET.

Potentially Saved
Engraved on are tombstones
Opened doors
But who's home
The sleeping whores
And left over chores
Prosthetic friends
And dummy humans

There's nothing for a person to live for
Just awaiting apocalyptic events
Like death and spiritual wars
Truths are in the scriptures and more
Soar eyes for sons that aren't able to hug mamas
And soar vags for daughters who's afraid to be a
gem.
Just survival of the stupidest

I guess that's the joke
That women and men don't see each other
Dehumanizing a plan
To defeat each other
A simple wish to start over
Just so we can re meet each other
Like Adam and Eve

It's okay not to be one another.
Taking are L's
But living in solitude
Knowing we failed
Even though god is our father too
We are not plastic surgery perfect
He made a reason for two
To live in this world n fulfill are purpose .
Yin yang we in the same spin
The colors of the wind
Black N white shows the purity and the sin
But instead we live in dividends
Kahooting with the same sex
And chatting in a shape of regret

We're potentially saved
And it's ashamed
I can't even express
That i love this man
Without someone speaking on his change
The change that Ching in between the pockets
Not how the physics of We
Got us on a rocket
Not The chemical bondage
Got me searching for some answers
And the loyalty in me
got me pursuing the unanswered.

where's summer?

Days like this
The summer feels cold
After my birthday there's
no fire to blow

I just want to scream at the world
Nd tell it to let me go
There are sad times when I told god
To leave me alone

I drown in the melancholy
This is a wish
Take me home to the love I miss
I'm too cold

This time I feel like loosing
It's like a honest pain that I feel like choosing
my head is gone

The love is rinked out
Like a rag
Small drips are dried ..
if he don't answer anymore
I tried
I have to leave this DOOR

IF YOU LOVE ME
PLEASE DONT OPEN ME ANYMORE

the day i left earth i asked for permission.

I can't wait to see the sky in Arizona wind
The birds are flying high
I see the beauty within
You keep me by your side then we'll share a grin
Spark something that takes us high
To another sin
"We are in a GEN
That can bring human race to a distance"
I laugh cause it sounds cute coming from your mouth
You scout the freckles upon my face
Then Gently rub my cheek
Run your hand smoothly down my waist
I peeped
Then you started to speak
Hey.
hi.
you okay ...?
umm I'm alright.
Sooo....
So what?
is this okay?

I had no option but to smile
You steady gawking at me
I feel like a gentle child
Who doesn’t know how to answer simple
Starting to feel insecure
Is he looking at my pimple
'Oh shut up, mind'
Just go with the tempo
I glanced and smirked and show off my dimple
I inhaled the aroma of our nightly weed
Exhaled the belief of being me
Then I looked at the sight of his hidden mole
That directed me to his lips
That’s when I lost control
To the fact that I laid a kiss upon them
He peeped
I started to speak
Hi.
Hey.
you okay ...?
Yeah I’m good.
Sooo....
So what?
is this okay?

suicide to the brain.

I would've call it love
But it was all a fake
Taking my only heart
Abuse my only fate

The last thing I ever wanted
us to do was
close this book
So I can start fresh like you did
And you won't answer my request
You won't even tell me how you feel
Like old times

Now I'm writing old rhythms
Nd feeling like porch chimes
Just swaying in the wind
Waiting for you to finish our journey
That were promised will take

But we're not married
Sometimes I wish I would've asked
But then again
I would've felt the mistake within
Cause what you did
Is what cause this torment

Look, I’m not asking you to save me
I just want you to know
That’s this is pure torture
Nd if I survive
Don’t ask for the hero’s autograph
Cause youll feel ashamed

And don’t hurt yourself
Because it’ll feel like suicide
To the brain
Some times I look at you
And all I see is pain
It’s written in your name
And I know you feel the blame
But the way you gambling
You have on your poker face
But all in due time
you’ll loose the game

Nd the only difference between
you and I
is I’ll still love you all the same ......

the thoughts that swayed.

It started
In my house
On the couch
Screaming for help
While you were so called
holding me down

Taking the women out of me
While I reached out
Stfu you said sooo sincerely
Making me silence my hurt
Your weight against my body
Equaled so much pain
Mentally, emotionally, physically
The only thoughts that's swayed

Was the first day I saw your smile
It's looked so promising and proud
I visioned nothing but us on the Milky Way
Learning to love and give joy
Then a dark cloud
Appears over our heads in action
Drops of rain falls down my face
You didn't notice
You never notice

Even when the lighting came
I was the only one who got struck
Then fucked in your cushion
you call a King Bed
Drowning in your
water wave sheet
Words of sorrow
Echoed in your voice
The fact that his happen everyday
It's like I have no choice
For the whips on my back
Are finally stained
The smile you crack now
Is only the preparation of my doom

I'm not choosing to see satan anymore
I'm not looking back
I'm trusting the direction to the door
As my heart starts to race to feel the freedom
I hear the deep footsteps of you reaching
I screamed as loud as a women begging for
peace within
He gives me a look that's stays
Reverses me to the thoughts that swayed

winter.

you make me feel like many things
I kissed you that night and I bet we got carried away
The passion between are eyes will fall far into stage
I'm taking your cold heart away
And baby I am bold
and Im strong
Are you the one for me
oh yes I know
And if you freeze forever and can't get your love together
I guess I have to find a coat.
Your heart was cold
the heartless code.

lightyear.

last lifetime ago
You where standing next to me
I couldn't have you for a reason
Time was a day to a season
You promised me a dance
But we didn't have a chance
To move different

Last lifetime ago
I remember your face
Your heart was big enough
to steer me your way

I know times fo
Last lifetime ago
I was in ah relationship I just could not let go
Yes you had to wait for me
and it came in your favor
You saved me the dance
And now we have a chance
to move different

Last lifetime ago
I remember your face
Your heart was big enough
My soul steered your way

COLORS EVERYWHERE.

LOVE YOUR PURPLE JACKET
IT STANDS FOR P
BUT I DONT THINK YOU UNDERSTAND
ME
MY MOODS ARENT FINAL
JUST THE FINALE INCREASE
IM MORE THAN PEACE
BUT IM DOWN TO PEICES
EVER SINCE I MET YOU
ITS LIKE THE WORLD IS DEFEATED
I DONT HATE YOU
BUT THE LOVE ISNT THERE
THATS NOT BAD
I JUST GOT MORE ROOM TO CARE
TO SHARE WITH YOU
COMPARE WITH YOU
SOMETIMES I FEEL LIKE YOU SCARED
TOO
THE WAY OUR FLARE GREW
IF I KNEW WHAT I KNEW TODAY
I WOULDVE BEEN HAD YOU.

COLORS EVERYWHERE
CANT EXPRESS THESE FEELINGS
USING ALL MY ADRENALINE

DISCUSSIONS EVERYWHERE
LIKE WE SPARING A CASE
GOD GIVEN TRUTH I JUST WANT TO END
THIS RACE.

CONFUSION EVERYWHERE
DONT KNOW WHERE TO GO
ITS SLOW WITH NO FLOW
BUT YOU WONT LET ME FOLD

DELUSIONS EVERYWHERE
NOT SURE IF ITS REAL
IS IT REAL?
JUST HAVE TO KEEP THE MOUTH
SEALED TO REVEAL.

bluetooth empath.

When I let you go
I know I will set free ..
But somehow when we meet again
I can't see

I mean historically speaking
The trust is broken
I try loving you but I cannot focus

Heated conversation
Lust in motion
I think of you as the devil's work
Just because Were chosen

Damn, I feel a connection
But I'm holding back
Thinking of the future..
cruise control in a Cadillac

Damn, I feel a connection
No cords attached
I think you know the feeling
My Bluetooth empath

Damn , do you feel it
Cause I'm spinning
Wish you were who you were
That's that crazy thinking

Damn , do you feel it
That girl you use to know
Walking tall like a women
But leaving in tip toe

Damn, I'm going to feel it
Shutting that door
Remembering the the love
Healing from the pain
Next time you see me
I won't be the same

Damn, then you'll feel it
But you won't go insane
Let be honest
We both was the blame
Two young kids trynna scrap the world
For some change
Basically you were speeding
And I was switching lanes
Trying to catch you
We crashed
I'm traumatized
Your paralyzed

Some how we'll race again
Not In this time
My Dear Lover Friend…

conquered.

I know what you came for
Take all of my paper
Came with all thoes weapons
Pulling off my necklace
Filled with seduction
Giving me the roughness
Yes I know I'm not yours
But in the end I'm conquered

I know where you came from
The women your not ashamed of
Who can love you in the open
These feelings are never spoken

But I'll say
that's okay
In the end I'm conquered

But no way
That's okay
In the end I'm conquered

WHY CHANGE?

I THINK ME AND YOU ARE JUST ALIKE
WE LET OUR FAMILIES CHOOSE OUR
FATES
INSTEAD OF OUR MINDS
WE ARE NEVER THE CAPTAINS OF OUR
SOUL
BECAUSE WE LET EVERYONE ELSE
DECIDE OUR LOADS

NOT DISAPPOINTING
JUST MISUNDERSTOOD

I GET IT, HONESTLY I DO
MANY PEOPLE ARE TALKING
AND NOT WATCHING
THE JURY HAS MADE ITS DECISION
UPON YOU

YOUR REPRESENTING THE LOYALTY OF
OTHERS
AND NOT YOURSELF
GROW PROPERLY
SO YOU CAN DECIDE YOUR OWN
BATTLES

HOW DO YOU WANT THE CHANGE BUT
NOT GIVE CHANGE
IF YOU TEACH HIM TO NOT BE LIKE YOU
THINGS WILL BE BETTER AND NOT THE
SAME
YOU ARE DEAF TO YOUR FAULTS
AND BLIND TO YOUR ACTIONS??

IM TRYING TO UNDERSTAND
INSTEAD OF DEFEND
BECAUSE WHAT YOU DID I CANT
COMPREHEND
I DONT SUPPORT IT BECAUSE IM TRYING
TO ESCAPE
YOU SAID YOU WAS TOO
WAS YOU LYING OR BEING A FAKE??

LISTEN TO ME CLEARLY
I WAS SENT TO YOU
CAUSE IM A ANGEL
PREACHING TO EVERYONE
SO THEY CAN EXCEPT YOUR ANGLES
WANT TO LET YOU KNOW YOUR LIFE IS
NOT JUST LIFE
YES, YOU HAVE A DAUGHTER, AND IN
THE FUTURE YOU HAVE A WIFE

I AM NOT MAD
JUST FURIOUS

CHANGE TO YOU IS DELIRIOUS
DONT HIDE YOUR PAIN
THROUGH YOUR EMPTY TEARS
YOU DONT CRY THE SAME
WHEN YOU LIE IN FEAR

DO YOU LOVE THE WAY YOU ARE
THROUGH A YOUR TIME FRAME?
IF YOU WONT STOP WHAT YOU CAUSE
THEN WHY CHANGE?

www.ingramcontent.com/pod-product-compliance
Lightning Source LLC
Chambersburg PA
CBHW051742130826
49812CB00033B/972
* 9 7 8 9 3 5 7 4 4 1 3 8 4 *